Between Hindsight and Foresight

Poems from My Walk

by
Leah Bailey

Poetry

Between Hindsight and Foresight
Poems from My Walk

First Printed in United Kingdom 2020

Published by Conscious Dreams Publishing
www.consciousdreamspublishing.com

Edited by Daniella Blechner

ISBN: 978-1-912551-98-9

Dedication

For my parents... who showed me how to walk anywhere I wanted to go... and for whose love I always come home...

Contents

Phantom Idea

Like a shadow or a shade it hangs there,
Waiting, slipping out of reach, just plagues me!
Why? How could I have lost something so rare?
Foolish mind, to have it, then let it free.
So happy a moment, so clear a day,
So precious a feeling lost to the night…
How could this bright spark have gotten away?
When each time it surfaced made me feel right.
Elusive and vital, I need it back!
Chasing and hunting, forever ahead!
I just know I'll be lost, all for the lack
Of this phantom idea weighing like lead.
     Suddenly, like dawn bringing us new light,
     I put down my pen; the verse is just right.

Journeys

It's 12 am, or so the clock bells chime,
I'm travelling off again, one more time…
Flying past places I don't remember yet,
and past people I have never met…

These are fast, old, familiar homes
past old familiar ways;
some new old places, here comes
the old newness of good days.

I don't know where I'm going,
and don't remember where I've been;
so this moment doesn't matter,
because it's all I've ever seen.

Suddenly it's a clear time to meet
anything and everything I've ever dreamed
before the moment passes, and I fear
that nothing is as it never seemed,
and where I want to be is still not near.

So in a beat, a heartbeat, I move
and forget the endless road's refrain.
I give the earth and path a shove
and lose whatever was new to gain.

Cause it's not about the road anymore…
To me the journey is for those beats…
Where I search internal land, sea and shore
for the place where the journey meets

with my life and within my mind.
Nothing full has been there,
the complete is hard to find
and on the journey you don't even care.

Life is all the moments, you often miss.
A journey of old remembered things,
a song, a house, a word, a first last kiss,
and that clock bell still rings and rings.

On the journey you will meet
moments that will scare you;
stop your heart and move your feet;
moments that will tear you.

But throughout the days, weeks and months,
when you don't won't know what or why,
they come to you in nameless fronts,
and life is about choosing to journey and try.

It's 12 am, or so the clock bells chime,
I'm travelling off again, one more time…
my choice.

How about you?

Broken Mask

I did what I was supposed to,
I did what was expected.
Band, choir, drama...
This and so much more I did.
To what end?
I listened to my teachers,
I listened to my friends,
I listened to problems,
I listened to pain...
But who listened to me?
Why should I not speak so much in class?
I won't then...
Why is it so strange that I want to be a minister?
Then I won't tell you that.
Why was it so strange I didn't always smile?
Well, I'll leave it painted there.
Why was it strange I get along with adults too?
Then I won't talk about that.
Why was it so strange I didn't cry too much?
Well, I'll shed a tear for you.
You, who never understood
Why I understood. I knew...
You knew I wrote poetry and fantasy.
You read it and said it was "good",
Wished "you could write like that"
Why would you wish that?
Don't you know pain caused that verse?
Don't you know the stories came from me?

My soul,
Which you never knew
Because you didn't ask.
I knew you,
I knew all that went on.
All seemed to talk to me...to tell me.
Who listened to me?
Choice few asked my pain.
Choice few knew I had any.
My life was "perfect"...
My advice was taken,
My time spent,
My dreams were made if not realized.
But who listened when I cried,
When I laughed,
When I spoke my soul?
You read my work and don't really know...
I knew.
I knew you all.
What I knew could have buried you.
Instead you buried me,
With many tears for your loss...of me,
Me who you never knew.
I lost my life, never really living for myself.
And I'm not the only one.
There are many unknown souls,
You do it to yourselves
And each other.

Don't write, "Loved one" on my piece of stone.
(You must be known to be loved)
My Epitaph? Paint it thus...
"Listen with your heart, don't just talk.
Listening gives you company, on life's walk.
No one wants to walk alone."
For though I walked with many...
No one walked with me.

The Dark Place

A gale from the depths of the soul that blows
Shaking and tearing your mind, end to end.
You enter a dark place everyone knows,
A place for no one, a place that will rend
Your soul piece by tiny piece into shreds,
A place that leaves you alone and afraid,
Sanity and will to live hang on threads,
Yet you have no strength, you can't beg for aid.
This place rips from you the world that you know,
You keep pain inside, though it seems too large,
You fear desertion, if you let it show,
Convince yourself to take it, stay in charge.
       Slowly you sink beneath the tide of night
       No one you know can see, or make it right.

After that, you know the dark place has you.
You're isolated again and again…
You feel stuck, like there's nothing you can do,
All that you feel every day is pain,
A wealth of sorrow, and fear, and darkness,
Total helplessness, you are so lonely,
See only a black abyss, its starkness,
Its depth so endless, you think 'If only….'
But there is no 'only', the grip, it holds,
Seizes you deep inside, you *want* to go,
You want to believe you can break its mold
You want to stand-up, scream and yell "please, no!"
       Slowly you sink beneath the tide of night
       No one you know can see, or make it right.

There's no fixing it, no way to deny
That you yourself, through self-pity and doubt,
Fell into the dark place, no matter why,
And closed all the doors, giving no way out.
No one there, reaching, to understand need,
How rejection constricts your heart and mind,
Things said often enough to plant the seed.
And comfort is never simple to find.
To all who don't know, it's called depression.
But the dark place is worse than most can fight.
It leaves the deepest scars, and impressions,
You only hope, pray, to survive the plight.
        Slowly you wait to escape the dark night,
        Waiting, waiting for an end, not in sight.

An Inner Strength

Whatever does not kill me
    serves only to make me stronger,
and for all I want to look away,
    I will stare that much longer.
Though the pain may bring down the darkest night,
I will look to myself... stand up and fight.

It may be hard and I may even fall,
but through the tears I will remember all.

One rock, be it large or small,
    can turn a mighty river's path
its rage must bend to the quiet stone,
    who stands, defies its wrath.
But it still flows on, despite all this change,
Possible improvement allows new range.

It may be hard and I may even fall,
but through the tears I will remember all.

One rock on my path, be it large or small,
    can't me stop for good.
If I trip on these rocks,
    I will think of only how I stood
up to rocks and their challenges before,
get up, dust off and keep striving for more.

It may be hard and I may even fall,
but through the tears I will remember all.

Because it never matters
        how many times in life you fall
or how long it takes you,
        every time, to face up to the strife.
It just matters that you got up at all,
and that you strive to continue your life.

It may be hard and you may even fall,
but through the tears you should remember all.

Many go through their lives
        thinking only of the things they've failed.
Things get overlooked;
        our self-image vision is so curtailed.
Remember that future ahead of you,
with your past always there to guide you through.

It may be hard and you may even fall,
but through the tears you should remember all.

Preserve it, for memories are things
        no one can take away,
let past triumphs and failures
        walk with you each and every day.
Rock or river, pass or fail, going, gone,
grab hold of your inner strength and move on.

It may be hard and you may even fall,
but through the tears you will overcome all.

Search for Truth

That which we know, we seek to disprove of.
We seek definition for hope, truth, and love,
But the search, in innocence begun,
means untruths, the facades have won.
Through pain and strife,
Through darkness and trust,
The trials of our life,
Greed, envy, and lust.
We do what we can and must do;
we see what we see, want to, believe it true.
But we can't prove a thing, no not one!
With all of the searching what can be done?
All of our lives we try to sift the true, the false...
Prove what we believe, and believe little besides.
Who can keep the innocent from such loss
for innocence is ruined amongst all the lies.
Knowledge and truth, one comes with the other,
innocence dies, protect them? Why bother?

Innocence

I want to know,
I don't want to be…
innocent.
I don't want to be told,
"don't worry about it",
or
"you don't understand".
I want to understand.
I want to know.
What it feels like
to touch,
to hold,
to feel someone…
near,
and all around.
I want to hear my name
whispered,
like a prayer
or
a wish.
I want to know all the joy
that others know,
at the touch
of a hand,
or lips,
gently pressed against
mine.

But can I banish
my innocence
without
the pain?
Can I feel the joy,
without
the sorrow?
Know,
without knowing too much
and being sorry
for losing the knowledge
of life without that pain?
Innocence is not *not*
knowing…
it is the unawareness
of the pain
required to know joy;
the sorrow,
required to know happiness.
Is the reason why
we are shielded in innocence
to be spared
the horrors
of knowing in full?
I guess I'm not
as innocent
as I thought…

Freedom's Feel

It's frightening here, new and large.
A place where I must be in charge;
where decisions made weigh down on me;
all my thoughts and actions seem
unnoticed by anyone, nor soon will be.
No pressure to change, it's like a dream…
…or a nightmare, if you can choose;
for now, what is there to lose?

Your self-respect, preconceived thought…
the rules and laws that always applied…
conformities, pressures…all at nought…
all the "gimmies", and how culture lied…
all fade away when the choice is yours.
Explore different places, on different shores.

Feel it happen when the first step is stepped,
feel it happen when you open your eyes.
The hope and ambition you always kept
released all at once, don't be surprised
when independence creeps in your heart
life on your own terms…it's time to start!

How Much?

written in the hope of youth

How much would you give to see
my deepest fears, my brightest dreams?
You seek them daily, pushing me…
an endless quest of yours this seems.
It goes on and does not slow or cease,
each weakness gives you lust for more,
and daily do your demands increase!
I can't escape what I adore,
those seeking eyes, that touch so sure.

You want it all, my soul my heart…
I don't know what my struggle's for!
Wanting someone to reveal all, a start
that I could finish when I chose,
a place to hide from constant fear,
someone in whom my sun both set and rose,
someone who would draw me near,
a flower without thorns coaxing me on.
You desire to know every piece of me?
I fear to tell you, turn in the morning and find you gone.
Will that be? Or will I see
Your smiling face every day?
How much would you give to see?
Would you let me tell you my way?
Would you stay there in the morning beside me?

Inferior Half

"I need you baby…" you say with a smile.
Yeah, we both know what you're after
And being fair we've known for a while.
Ignore the sound, just every woman's laughter.
You think you're the King, suave and hot…
Hate to break it to you boys… you're not!
We try to be subtle only to find that you
are denser than bricks with less of a clue.

To get you to understand we're interested in you,
We have to practically sit in your lap.
Though we give you every hint we can think to,
Your aloof mystery turns out to be oblivious sap.
You think we're your slaves, "Back to the kitchen!"
But when you want some "fun" you're just itchin'…
Piling on the sweet words of false praise,
All you really want from us is a raise.

Yeah right, I'm so sure, I can't work that way!
You want some from us you have to be true.
The sweet and sincere, has to be every day.
Gotta know you love us, and we've got to believe you.

Don't tell us it's love, when you think it's not.
We're not possessions, don't parade us for your friends.
Don't tell intimate secrets, and don't claim you just forgot
The important things, we'll show you the door when it ends.
We're the "dumber sex", but diamonds are our best friend.
Dogs are yours, now what kind of message does that send?
Intelligence isn't your strong point, and it doesn't seem to grow,
If you're interested, *if* you're worth it, well…we'll let you know.

Tender Rain

In the hazy lazy early morning light,
chill air brushes my skin.
You tuck-up the covers
before wrapping me in your arms again.
The sky pours whispering rain down the window,
the sound rustles in with the wind
along with that chill draught sipping,
Kissing the leaves of the trees.
The sound, the caressing breeze, the rain is tender...
after the love we have made.
I feel no chill, entwined in your branches,
your hands caress me, tender as that breeze,
your skin warms me from the air,
and your whisper concerts with the rain;
Tenderly, 'I love you, thank you, you are wondrous.'
We turn in bed, change places, but never let go.
Your arms circle me, my leg holds you,
I lay my head on your chest and feel at home,
and the rain whispers down the window sill.
You kiss me and hold me, and again we begin to move.
Slow and tender, loving, joining, in an old rhythm
With the rain.
I sigh, afraid the rain will stop,
fearing to break the spell, I murmur your name.
You whisper your love...
In the afterglow of our motion I can still hear
Your voice on the wind, kissing the window
Spilling over my skin, warming my soul.
This feeling fills me completely
With the rain pouring down
Tenderly...this moment...I have made a memory.

Losing My Senses

I watch my lover sleeping, when his eyes are closed.
He looks so peaceful, handsome, a pure light.
He watches me, above him, lovingly reposed.

I sense him near, sweet sweat in the bed clothes,
he smells my hair, fallen to his right,
I watch my lover sleeping, when his eyes are closed.

I feel his caress, down my face and my side it flows,
we feel our skin touch and he holds me tight.
He watches me, above him, lovingly reposed.

I taste his lips, salty-sweet, light and posed,
he tastes my skin, cheek and neck, a featherweight.
I watch my lover sleeping, when his eyes are closed.

I hear his whisper in my ear, as he pulls me close,
he listens to my sighs and my heart pounding in flight.
He watches me, above him, lovingly reposed.

The sense beyond senses holds me the most.
Our love, in calm moments, goes beyond all sight…
As I watch my lover sleeping, when his eyes are closed,
he watches me, above him, lovingly reposed.

Out of Sight

I take a trip to rest my mind.
Now I'm home and I seem to find
That you haven't left me at all.

You're not here but yet you are.
Out of sight but *in* control.
From my thoughts you're never far.
Reminders so often, take their toll.

I think of you, and smile quickly.
You float in and out, so slickly.
Without your voice I still hear your call.

In my thoughts, when you are gone, you're still bright.
Never out of mind, though you're out of sight.

Without

I feel the emptiness beside…inside me,
An empty full heart and bed today.
I wonder, disbelieving, how this could be?

I remember your caress gentle and carefree,
how you touched me body and mind, every way.
Yet I feel the emptiness beside…inside me.

Our love was so bright, no one could see.
With joy, so unending, I used to say,
"I wonder, disbelieving, how this could be?"

Recalling that wonder I send out a plea,
"Please God, take this pain I pray!"
Now I feel the emptiness beside…inside me.

To raise to such heights, finally free!
Then crash to such depths, oh! How I sway,
and wonder, disbelieving, how this could be?

Without your love I may wither and bleed.
So far, so very unbelievably far away.
I feel the emptiness beside…inside me…
I wonder, disbelieving, how this could be?

Unseen

The mask I wear to hide from you
holds back the ache in due course,
all you see is the daily smile;
each smile is getting worse.

You don't know the want, the need, here.
I feel it with each flash of those eyes
falling on mine; feel so desperate
to let fall my fatal disguise.

I paint my face to hide the dark
circles… for lack of sleep
makes my dreams of you nightmarish,
full of empty despair, wide and deep.

Your eyes, pass on…still don't see;
fleeting wishes that last days,
constant while I struggle, *need*,
to have you by my side in all ways.

Stalking

Eyes burning, fire… sparkling bright
coals within the depths of night.
Passion flows, erratic breath, muscles tense,
heart race, energy high and heightened sense.
See the tigress, stalking through
Jungle steam and heat…
she's looking just for you;
steady, steady, steady drum beat.
Pounding through, shivering sweat…
She's still not done yet.
Muscles ripple, gasp, grasp, grip,
biting shoulder, neck, leg, lip;
peeling clothes, ripping, shred,
Fear, excitement, mix and twine.
Not a whimper nor a word be said,
groan and hold tight the vine.
You are caught, she holds you there.
Climbing, climaxing, swoon, swear,
call to God, rapture, rising, round,
claws, calls, growls, frightening sound.
Then the calm, the sigh… relax…
held and soothed and gently kissed.
From climbing heights now collapsed
breath escaping in a hiss.
Softly, slowly pads away,
the tigress at the break of day.
Rest easy in tired slumber
wake alone and in wonder.
When will you be stalked anew
Will the tigress stalk again?
If she does, will she choose you?
Or will only memory remain?

Artists in a Bar

I have this place I go
to write, quiet or crazy…
It's a good place…
staff who know I'm a regular,
Decent food decent drinks…
enough to blow through
the writer's blocks.
A new musician begins,
I'm used to the other,
good tunes, knows his stuff,
sweet voice, good guitar.
I guess I wasn't paying attention.

Then the first notes hit,
and now a smile spreads
unbidden and unstoppable
across my face,
I recognise the intro…
Everyone singing along
is a decade too young…
so is the piano player, but…
as he catches my eye across the bar,
sees that recognition,
knows I know the tune,
I suddenly don't care…
what's a decade anyway?
In that moment of recognition,
two artists in a bar.
I throw my head back and laugh.

Another regular beats me to the punch
of buying him a drink…
maybe later, if he wants one?
The conspiracy continues
as I recognise intro after intro
singing along and smiling
appreciation; I'm still searching
trying to nail down my idea…

Then it hits me… two artists
in a bar,
eyes meet the first few notes
and now a smile spreads
unbidden and unstoppable…

Prey

I want to be prey, in the dead of a dark night
I want to be pursued and hunted, shadowed and sought
With the avidity of a starving, ravenous appetite
With the desire of a prize, a battle long fought.
I need to be prey, an object of pure urgency and rapture,
I need to be pursued with every intention of capture.

I would submit to the savagery of Zeus as so many before.
Like Leda and Io, or Demeter my siren's call would be clear
His desperate pursuit to possess their beauty and more
Gives me chills of fervour and heat without a trace of fear
I would submit to desire that moves heaven and earth
To one such as Zeus going to great lengths to show my worth.

I could burn like the Carthage queen, on a fire I myself caged
I could be consumed, exhausted, devoured in the passion
With the flames licking bare flesh with a seductive, wanton, rage
Slave to a fevered frenzy, a dire hunger for any ration
I could burn in the sultry, steaming thrill coveted by the soul
I could be consumed in throes of agony, ecstasy of the whole.

I should succumb like Persephone to the ravishment of hell
I should thirst for the temptation to be the obsession of a God
Eating the profane seeds of the carnal, drawing a bottomless well
Inviting intoxication to stir longing and weaknesses flawed
I should succumb to worshipping the itch of entangled lust
I should thirst for Hades' yearning till its force turn me to dust.

I dream of Gweneviere's affliction, the impulse to cave
Inclined to devotion whilst desiring the forbidden affair
To have a good and loyal man wed, yet still you crave
To give in to the champion, the knight, and to not care
I dream the ardour of my knight's fascination, though bound
Inclined to rash abandon, being ever lost and ever found.

I fear for Helen's power, of violence's energy released,
I know the anxious elation that destroys a world for want
The animal lash of wrath, its ferocity ever increased
By the heat of wild excitement, eager battle on every front
I fear the exaltation of battle dominating all my senses
I know the alluring power of the physical breaking all defences.

I want to be prey, aroused by the pursuit of passion's wake
I want the hunt that creates a game where all is won or lost
With the inevitability of defeat and ravenous just to take
And give in the erotic dance of ecstasy at whatever the cost
I want to hunt and be hunted, pure or violent, hunger and need,
I want to burn and consume, to submit and crave, to chase and lead.

How much?

written in the knowledge of an adult

How much would you give,
to re-run that first kiss?
How much would you do,
to be first time lovers again?
How much just to live,
remembering all the things you miss?
How much just to go,
back where your love might still remain?

Would you give everything,
to keep what you once had?
Would you give anything,
not to feel it hurt so bad?
Watching your heart bleed on the floor
would you catch the tears?
Watching your love walk out the door
would you see your worst fears?
Would you give everything
to keep what you once had?

How much do I wish you'd come home
and smile that same smile from the first?
How much would I give to hold you close
without feeling like my own arms are chains?
How much I hate lying next to you alone?
Routine to hide the pain is the worst...
How much the soothing drug and the dose?
How long before you tell me we're all done?

I would give everything
to keep what we once had.
I would do anything
to not feel it hurt so bad.
How much I want you back here with me
to pick my bleeding heart off the floor.
How much I want you and I to be
as much in love as we seemed to be before.
I would give everything
to keep what we once had.
I would do anything
to not feel it hurt so bad.

Pieces in Parts

First Piece

Piece by piece falls away
Placed, packed, carried
Away into the van to go…
Leaving emptiness behind.

Bit by bit the reality
sinks into my mind,
and into my heart,
too real by a good bit.

Box by box unloaded
into an empty flat,
piles mounded around,
containers containing it all.

Room by room I arrange,
unpack, unbox, unfold
pieces of the past,
while the future shatters.

Shard by shard I'm cut
on the edges of soul
and heart laying in boxes
broken and randomised.

Minute by minute I move
through each piece
of things connected
to disconnected memory.

Hour by hour distracted
by ordering the space,
half heartedly failing
avoiding an empty heart.

Moment by moment passes,
do, finish, carry on,
next piece, and more…
till its done, as I am.

Memory by memory I look,
search, for a chance,
reason and hope;
grains gathered in desperation.

Thought by thought
the pieces come together
nothing remains,
anything is possible.

Second Piece

So many pieces to place,
So much time to fill,
So much life to build
Endings and beginnings.

Day by day a year goes,
so short, and still long.
Mind and heart so different,
Hardly know what's real.

The broken pieces start
to fit together again,
knit together again,
into something new.

Rooms are no longer
empty or new to me,
now they hold
memories slow built.

Now they hold
what I have become,
still mending the shape
just around the edges.

No longer as sure
of what the shape is...
I think I like it...
but still incomplete.

A piece of me is ok
with being incomplete,
a piece of me is not.
Angry, frustrated, impatient.

I'm tired of road building,
too many goddamn
pieces
that don't fit anywhere.

Some pieces don't
fit anymore,
which is both good,
and bad.

Because those pieces
also don't fit in a box,
won't go away,
no matter how I arrange.

Those pieces stare
and sit stubborn,
waiting for resolution;
can't hide them.

My mind refused
to lock them
away,
so they gather dust

waiting for some other
to tell me where to
put them, finally.
So I and they wait.

I find new pieces
to my new pictures,
enjoy each addition
and forget old ones.

Till I come home,
my new piece of
home and life
and the old stares from a corner.

Days I want to
smash the old
beyond repair
beyond any renewal.

Days I want the
pieces of the past
to weave with the new
to make it complete.

I hate my piece of
limbo, that box
of left over pieces
with unresolved edges.

Nothing remains
of hopes I once had.
The picture is new
I want more than before…

Anything is possible
still, but I can't
wait forever for clarity…
I'll go to pieces!

Third Piece

Not moving the pieces
around the bored board
not anymore
not again…

A two year piece
of my existence.
Getting papercuts
on mislaid pieces,

mislaid memories,
almost forgotten…
almost resolved…
almost put away…

No place in the picture
For almost anymore.
Nor old pieces
of old pictures…

Time to let them go,
let them fade,
slip into a box,
packed away in past.

These pieces are, *were*,
important, needed…
but no longer.
They have changed shape.

Not to be forgotten,
but to be kept, fitted
where they belong,
in old pictures of before.

Before I found myself,
before I found new place,
before I found peace,
in my own skin,

in my own self,
in my own needs,
in my own wants,
in my own picture,

of the pieces I want,
need, and have
fitting into place
in my own future.

Laying the pieces
one by one
day by day
in front of me;

enjoying the new shape,
the new picture
and looking at a piece
of the horizon.

Each time I finish
a solid row
the edges change,
the directions change.

I know that
the missing pieces
will arrive,
and I don't miss

the old pictures
as much
as I used to
anymore.

I have set
the pieces free...
old, new and
all the ones in between.

Old will fade
and not cut me,
new will multiply
and solidify.

The fuzzy edge
doesn't scare me.
My piece of sky,
My developing picture.

Everything is possible
once again;
and one thing
is finally certain:

I'm not going to pieces
ever again,
and I'm hungry
for the next piece of life.

Connecting

If you've time, in London Waterloo,
go upstairs, next to coffee and pigeons.
Look down, especially weekday evenings,
and see the great heart pumping with life.
I'm amazed, overwhelmed, aghast…
all those people, strangers, in proximity.
I know it's 'not done' and all but I think:
Should I say hello to the parent next to me,
checking a train I know how to locate?
Should I pass a subtle tissue to the girl
reading her texts, as I have before?
Should I stand in the way of the guy,
getting aggressive, and pretend
my headphones…are on…?
Should I share a smile with the lady
across from me,
at the person next to me,
nodding off over a video…?
The overflow of conversation
waiting to be had, bubbles to my lips.
I can't stop it, looking down on
the flow of chaos. I wonder
how many of them, have lives I
should know, would know, could know?
How many would want to know me?
Is it so bad, dipping hands
into the stream of humanity
see if someone grabs hold,
as a needed, wanted contact.

Kindness of strangers
reaching out to stop being strange,
why not?
When did we become isolated
in a crowd?
When did we turn blind
to suffering it costs nothing to
alleviate?
If you've the time, in London Waterloo,
go upstairs, next to coffee and pigeons...
Look down, especially weekday evenings,
and see the great heart pumping with life...
Then look left
and start talking...

Define Alone...

Is it an empty restaurant
with kind staff who smile,
and remove the other set
so you don't feel alone?

Is it the abandoned
and crumbling petrol station
with an exit sign the only
legible sign
through flimsy wire fence?

Is it the dim twilight
painting pastel colours
as your steps echo
on cracking pavement
one set?

Is it the lone voice
of your nature
turning thoughts
like straw into gold
giving you someone
to talk to?

Is it the single flame
burning on the tea light
next to your single
glass of wine?

Is it an empty night
staring out a window
which frames a twisted,
ivy covered tree
in the gathering night
with emerging stars?

Is it closing your eyes
and wiggling your toes
in the wet sand
feeling the wash
of the grit begin to
sink you
in the last warmth
of summer?

Is it a single touch
along the jawline
thoughtful
gentle
provoking thoughts
of it being
someone else's
hand?

Is it a strand
of long hair

in your eye
shifting the light
into a forested
shadow?

Is it an empty chair,
staring,
sitting across
the table
wanting to be
filled?

There is so much that
can seem alone
but alone... is not
the same,
as lonely...

I relax into the empty
the abandoned and
crumbled
the dim twilight
the turning thoughts
the single flame
the single glass
the wooden frame
the twisted tree
the closed eyes
the sinking sand
the last warmth
the single touch
the long hair
the empty chair.

I listen to the alone...
and am content.

Company

Sometimes what you want,
is the avid, attentive company of
someone affectionate
someone who gazes in your eyes
doesn't see anyone else
in the room, in the bar,
in the world...

Sometimes what you want
is the company of the raucous,
the rowdy, the hell-raising
crowd of friends
both hilarious
and simultaneously
embarrassing
in the best way possible...
company to count on
for crazy, for distraction,
for anything that doesn't
make sense.

After you may want the company
of the vengeful, the wrathful
of friends, offended
on your behalf...
experts in plotting,
in tissues and ways
of raging that somehow
calm your soul with sisterhood.

And most times the continuous
company that comforts
in both quiet and conversing
whose peaceful and companionable
silence is calming in a way
the riling company could never be
someone who says
as much in silence
as those in cacophony.

As in all things…
it's the company that counts.

Must Be Somewhere

AHH! Where is it!
Honestly! Not today...
Where is that file?
Hours of work,
Down the drain...
Promotion, admiration,
Respect...
Out of the window...
Really... and my pass,
Finding the file is useless
Without my pass key...
Building security
May know me,
But won't let me in...

Keys, keys, keys...
Where did I see
Those last?
Regret throwing
That beeping thing
Out the window
Now,
But the dog bark
Was setting it off
At all hours...
I know I put them
Down, after last night
Right next to my
Earrings..now,

Where did they go?
Aww, come on,
My mother gave me
Those hideous
Things, and insisted
I wore them
Last night,
Maybe I'm not
Sorry to lose
Them, but not
me keys!

That tone, I know
That tone, losing it
Bit by bit,
My own teeth
Grating, fighting
Losing my patience
As well as my
Tone, why can't
They listen?
Why can't they learn?
All I want to do
Is help them,
Pass their test,
Learn their text,
Feel a love
Of literature…
Why? How! Did

44

I lose their
Attention?
How did I lose
Their respect?
All I did was care,
All I did was try
To teach, what
They could learn.

Where was I?
Oh yes, trying
Not to lose
My voice, just
One stray thought
One missed chance
And it's almost
Impossible
To find my way
Back,
Maybe a night away,
Lose some time,
Lost in thoughts,
Lost in where
I wanted to be,
Instead of where
I am before
I lost my way.

And the seat,
The one I always
Choose gone,
How?
I left my coat,
Left my book
Conveniently moved
When I stepped
Away
Just for a
Moment,
So unfair,
So inconvenient
Rude, when
Did such a loss
Of manners
Happen
When did we lose
Our concern
For treating others
As we
Wish to be
treated?

I must be somewhere,
I must have left it,
Between the night

And the morning...
The will to fight,
For the dreams
Of my past,
Some little girl dreams
Some a woman's wish.
When did I lose my
Tongue,
To speak up,
For myself, for what
Is important to me,
For what I
Don't want
To lose or leave
Unattended?

It must be here somewhere,
The memory of why
The future, looked
So bright, so full
Of promise.
I know I kept them
Next to the earrings?
Or the keys?
Or the beeping thing?
Out the window,
With my mind...

That means digging,
Deep, in the dirt
Beneath the window
Hoping
It's not buried
With my heart
And soul.
Which I'm sure
I left
Somewhere safe
When the battle
To keep track
Got lost
With the files,
And images
Pictures of friends
Lost
Ideas and memories
Of love
Lost
I'm still sure
I'm just forgetting
Something simple,
I'm sure they'll turn
Up
It's always
The last place
You look.

How do I Accept?

Day to day is not so bad
As it can sometimes feel,
Lack of some desires can make you mad
But most of the want isn't real.

Perspective just eludes me,
I battle myself heart and mind,
What I have goes as far as I can see,
Yet my want is stuck on what I can't find.

Why can't I accept, what I'm given?
Why can't I accept, what is here?
Why must my heart and mind be riven
Over a nebulous need so unclear?

Why can I not see what others do
Within myself? What might draw
What I want to me, give me some clue,
To accept I'm worthwhile and may fall

Yet into what I most need to complete
My ever present search and greed,
And stop this destructive trend to complete
With what is and what should be that feeds

My discontent with a life so well lived…
How do I pause, take stock and revel
In what kind fate has always gives
How do I accept and keep myself level?

Take the Dog for a Walk

I know it's raining and darker sure
But if we don't get out
He'll do nothing but bark, I'll shout
Till neither of us can take any more.
Water on my cheeks, not a good start...
Dog lead pulls me this way and that,
Sometimes I wish he'd stop to bark at a cat,
Soaking to the skin not too small,
I guess, I just thought I'd try...
Before dinner sat too well to go
Too far from the couch you know?
You should go but you wonder "why"?
Dog gets loose, out of my self-control,
Chasing it, shushing it, constant ask...
Feel like sitting in my bar and task
It to someone else to patrol.
I don't have the energy for it, all the time...
So,...damn... needy, it never leaves off,
Begging for attention at the slightest cough,
Attention drawn I can only pretend it's not mine.
Believe me, I'd ditch it, dump it, if I could.
But I'm stuck feeding it, walking it,
In rain and sun, when it's dark or lit,
Looks like I'm living with this dog for good.

Date With Myself

Heya, it's been a while
  Yeah, I know sorry
It's fine I just want a smile
  No need, seriously, to worry
Worry? Me, why would I?
  You can't fool me you know
I just hate seeing you cry
  I told you I needed to go.
Too tempting I guess
Staying at home is no good.
  I never loved you any less
  I know, I would accept if I could.

Maybe someone will join us
You never can tell,
You might see a new trust
And then feel well
  That seems unlikely now
  You know how my luck's been
  I will no longer stop and bow
  Too many let downs I've seen
Oh, come on, you're not past
That need or that sight
Besides I'm here, first to last
I'll never leave the light
  Not sure that helps me
  Not like we're in love either
No matter what we see
Things we can't do neither.

I can love if you let me
     Good but not enough
I know how to set you free
     It will get too tough
No it won't I'll always be here
     Undoubted but, I mean really…
If not me, who else can care?
     Needs someone else, nearly.
No you don't you need only you
     Suppose I can't argue with myself
If you do at least it's all true,
     No point in leaving it all on the shelf.

Wash My Hair

Honestly, didn't I just?
It's too long, tangles.
AARGH! never behaves,
straight when I want curl,
curls when I want straight,
wavy when I want anything else.

I should cut it.
Should I cut it?
Why don't I cut it?
Cutting it won't help,
sigh…
The rest of the package…
seems to be wanting.

The paint job, sloppy,
mismatched,
never did get it right.
Who has time?
The dress, too tight,
will anyone know
in the dark of the bar?
Will they care?

Who knows thin, curvy,
front loaded, back loaded,
need a consultant
in marketing,
just to follow
the packaging guidelines…
what a mess.

Now, really? now…
the brush won't even
go through that knot.
In my hair,
and my stomach.
Maybe a diet?
What's, what's her name…?
What's she on now?
Does it work?
Could it change it?

Aargh…! The phone?
What? Go out? A date?
sorry…I'm… uh…
washing my hair.

Boots in the Lamplight

Walking along here
Late at night
City sounds so clear
In lamplight.

On the gummed sidewalk
Pair of shoes,
That can almost talk,
Who could lose?

Boots with crumpled tops
Falling o'er
Scuffed and left to drop
On night's floor.

Where might they have gone
Without these?
Left out here alone
Me to tease…

Cinderella tale?
Or drunk loss?
Eaten by a whale?
Wire cross?

They are a bit small,
Dwarf maybe?
Grown a bit too tall?
Toes must free?

They are a bit old,
Witches tread?
But will she be cold?
Or just dead?

A giant's last meal,
Just a snack,
Leaving just the heel
Leather tacks.

Cars pass me by fast
While I think
Theories that don't last
Pass in blinks.

One pair of shoes left
Night time pause
lamplight is bereft
idea claws.

Fascinating me
This lost pair
Why can't I just see?
Lost in air.

Where have they gone to?
From where come?
My fancies are true,
I go home.

Everyone Else

In the crowded
Noisy bar
Everyone else
Is with
Everyone else.

Groups gather
With laughter
And chat
And romance
And gossip
And drinks
And domestics
And break-ups
And get-togethers
Everyone else,

But me.

But I'm still
Here
With everyone else.

In the bar
In the noise
Apart from
and a part of
their noise
their smiles
their gossip.

"Who is that girl?
Dressed for a date,
But all alone?"
Me, enjoying the
Energy...
And cocktails
(Two for one)
I don't have
To share.

I let the sound
And the music
And the life surround
Me,

I feel it on my skin
vibrate life,
That I'm still part of...
Alone or not.

Why not?
Why not live
In the background
Of others' living?
Aren't we all?

Just because
They don't sit
With me,
They don't know
Me,

Doesn't mean
We aren't connected.

We all chose this
Place,
We all chose this

Time,
Why not? Why?

Everyone else
Has been where
I am.
Everyone else knows
What
I know.

Life is noisy
And laughter
And gossip
And romance
And heartache
And drinks
And chat
And domestics
And get-togethers,
Why break it up?
Aren't we all...

Everyone else...?

Remember that...

Remember that time
We went swimming late
At that party with...
Oh, what's his name?

Remember that sleepover,
With make-up and hair,
Done to 80's fashion...
Or was it 90's?

Remember school dances
Where tears and laughs
Were had by all...?
Except the recurring ex.

Remember colours week?
A week of school war,
Months of practice,
For victory that meant little and all.

Remember friends, good and bad,
Old and new, didn't matter...
Trips and trials,
Tears and smiles.

I forgot how much
Time had passed...
Since last we sat
And remembered.

I forgot how much
I shared with you,
That no one else
Ever knew.

I forgot the joy
Of remembering all
The things that seemed
To matter more.

I forgot to forget,
(And never will again)
What I have been
Makes me who I am.

Part Time Prison

Six am on a Monday morning
Although we'd much rather be snoring...
ERR...ERRR...ERRR goes the alarm.
You'd think those inventors could
Find us a sound with more charm.
Groggy, must do what we should...
Get up, get dressed, all hygiene,
Stretch, put on what smells most clean.

Walk down the street in hot September air,
On the corner with the other inmates.
No one's awake and no one seems to care,
Big yellow transport never hesitates
To come late, make you stand a bit longer,
Leave you to wish your coffee was stronger.
Boarding the bus you head to your cracked seat,
It jerks, bumps to a start before you sink,
You crowd into a spot someone new yet to meet...
They're an asylum escapee you think.

You reach the prison walls, they're cold and mean,
Windows that don't open, the stairs obscene.
Find your first torture session, you must run...
Being late asks for a fate worse than death,
If the torturous classes are no fun...
Have late study hall and you'll shoot yourself.
Math first, joy of joys, the witch of the west,
And if she's this bad just think of the rest!
History, English, Chemistry and then,
It's time to leave prison, with all the tomes,
180 days o'er again
Just because our parents don't want us home.

Voiceless

Imagine…
What would you do
What would you think
If your voice
Was in fact
Voiceless?

If when you spoke
You felt
Speechless?

If you poured
You heart
And mind
And soul
Into every
Word…
Like tears.

Only to have them
dashed away,
like all you had
spoken…
was
worthless.

What if you fought
every day,
for just
for a moment.
Just one.

Where you
Had
A voice
That was heard.
That mattered…

That you didn't feel
Like you were shouting
Into something
As empty
As you felt
When others'
Ears
Heard
But didn't
Listen…

Voiceless
Once again…

Freedom's Judgment

How dare you tell me that I feel no pain?
More chances, more choice, than ever before,
Just because war's blood is not in my reign.

What of the pressures that my days contain?
The expectations the world does implore?
And still you tell me that I feel no pain?

Obligations I must daily maintain.
The status of outcast threatens more and more,
Despite that war's blood, on me, does not rain.

Suicide brings us down if we cannot gain.
Our life's blood, in success' dreams we pour.
Still you dare tell me that I feel no pain!

My life's a whirlwind; I'm caught in the frame
society designed, they control the core.
Even though war's blood is not on my rein.

You give choiceless choices, I am so constrained.
Each day I die from life that much is sure.
How dare you tell me that I feel no pain?
Just because war's blood is not in my reign.

SEE

Eye said see!
Look, look at me!
What? What is there?
Cold? Sharp? Beware!
Warmth? Hope? Good day...
Now, what can I say?

Eye said see!
Okay! Let it be?
Never, need to know,
Don't let ignorance grow.
More understood
Means more for good.

Look, look at those!
What we think grows
With each new view...
Who, who sees you?
Learn what you can
The gaze of man.

Ignorance breeds
When no one seeds
The view of each
The gaze can't reach;
Why not try more
Until you are sure?

See The Moment

Through the mad rush of the day
We frequently forget ourselves.
One glance at the sky, a breath just to say,
Sunrise or sunset brings calm that quells.
Our eyes miss the escaping coloured view,
Passing glances at watches, too much to do!
We miss warm gold, royal purple and blue;
We miss painted clouds, natural, pure and true;
Music embedded in hues, brush strokes in the sky.
But our alarms and reminders continue to fly,
the day burns clear because of sunrise light,
the sunset heralds a deep dream filled night.
Why would God create such views in our sight?
We undeserving people, who's busy lives keep us in flight?

Worshiping Lethe

Unpredictable and full of chaos,
splashes from Lethe divert the mind,
sensations; sight, sound and scent... no loss.

A little thing can take you across.
It's a moment or 20 years that you find;
unpredictable and full of chaos.

Diamonds undimmed in all the dross,
nothing left to die, thoughts are kind
sensations; sight, sound and scent... no loss.

Random is its strength, purely a dice toss,
find what you didn't know you need, lined,
unpredictable and full of chaos.

First summer campfire to the last winter frost,
teenaged dreams and loves too far behind.
Sensations; sight, sound and scent... no loss.

Worshiping Lethe, immortal with flaws,
live as long as memory intertwined.
Unpredictable and full of chaos,
sensations; sight, sound and scent...no loss.

Diamonds

Afraid to speak, in case my breath shakes,
Hanging in the cool air, in the dark.
Sweep the ceiling with light and they wake…
a million, star-like, liquid diamonds spark.
The guide shares tales of its past,
these tunnels that saved a town from war,
their words carved in walls, seem to last
long past their carvers, deep in cliffs core.
Dew drops in coal black, condensed cold
tremble as we press, touch and reform
with each new breath, new visit, tale told,
bravery and humour, heroic acts preformed
by a people on the coast. As bombs fall,
bakers feed, trains supply, caverns care
for souls as numerous as the droplets fall,
diamonds on stone, waiting to flare.

The Eyes of Walls

Painted and frozen
No choice but to look
At all that passes
Before their face.

Panels of motion
Caught by the brush
Each a different
Point of view.

Children forever wait
Looking out at snow,
Stag forever jumps
Away from hound jaws.

Rooster forever crows
With silent hoarse voice,
Birds of many kinds
Fly off forever, nowhere.

What they must see
In their frozen time
Of time forever passing
Brushing the brush strokes.

Pairing them in place,
Voices of great men,
Love of great women,
Gossip of high society,

Wretchedness of poor,
Dancing and joy,
Deeds of darkness,
and inspiration to light.

Simple scenes
Grown more complex
By all that they
Have seen and known.

To ask these walls,
To hear their tales
Beyond time, through it
Stand in awe of it...

To know I'm only
A moment, a thought,
Brief lit and gone
Past the eyes of walls.

Night Watch

Night time has a thousand eyes
The daytime has but one
Night's is ever pursuing
Those who's light is lies.

They leave the light and seem to fade…
Doing wrong in the day they flee
From the indistinguishable masses
Thinking, in error, to find shelter in shade.

The guard is a ruse, for the night to feed
On the souls of those alone,
Of those who do evil to hunt
In all the known darkness, vengeance freed.

Night knows the shadows, all,
Moon and stars shine on unsuspecting faces
Fooled into exposure of their sins,
Condemned forever to a nightmare fall.

Night will haunt their sleep…
The sun would be a blessing
Burning off maybe, but in the dark
You can't hide from yourself the secrets you keep.

Fear

Beside you.
Black rose in the garden,
Black sheep in the fold,
Beast without recall,
Beast of tales untold.
Who dares block thy path?
Who dares risk thy wrath?
Vanity, sloth, and greed…
Three vices of the seed.
Gluttony, wrath, and lust…
Three more for dust.
But blasphemy the worst
Of all the vice's thirsts.
The snake tempts man
Any way he can.
Be afraid my son,
Until the race is won.
Take a bite, if you dare
Of the devil's share.
Remember six seeds
Is all he needs
To keep you.

Get Real

In this era we question, answer's always the same.
Why it's such a mystery, elusive, a thing we can't name.
"This is real…" or "the reality is..", "come on, get real."
Things we say, every day, said when we rarely feel.
What is real to me, may not be, never be, to you.
It could be your actions or ideas you think true,
So many times it seems our dreams come through;
Guess that means dreams can be reality too.

You say, "I know what's real!" sure you do, think so?
Seems all must see the same, to be real you know?
Not what it's cracked up to be, only what we make it.
Only if your heart and mind completely fit.
Transfer is rare, and only the basics for free…
Concepts that we and me and she and thee all see.
Like beauty, truth, peace, love even then…
We forever redefine and strive for these things when

Others tell us to "get real" and we scream "NO!" back.
Hopes and dreams are only real when time is all we lack.
How else do we grow, aim for the unrealistic, attain?
The struggle, the failures are where we get real gain,
Strike for the best, wait for the rest, only for time and trial
Relax into the "reality" of today, tomorrow's can wait awhile.

I'm Coming Back As A Cat

What is this thing,
m... m... mor... ning?
Sorry, I don't think
I can get that
into my vocabulary.
Oh! Wait, I know!
That's that time
When the sun
comes up...
and you
are being lazy,
and not feeding me
fast enough.
It's annoying you
know, to have to
keep padding
and bumping
your face 'till
you get to it...
inconsiderate,
Really...

Afternoon is for waking,
briefly, to shift,
from one sun spot
to the next,
the sun moving is
so....glorious.

The heat of the couch,
the bed, the paving,
it's such a joy
to sleep wherever I am.
Streeeeeetch out,
every limb
every finger and toe,
fur sprawled across
a pool of sunshine;
warmth soaks into
every fluffy inch.

I'll need a bath soon…
No! Not water…
Who do you think I am?
The *dog*?
So undignified, splashing
and snorting in some sudsy mess
Yuck! My tongue will do…
Much neater, much cleaner.
My spine lets me reach
all parts, twist
and turn, paws in the air…
Oh how superb
to not be confined
to be so flexible
I can fit
comfortably
anywhere, any which way.

Hey! What's that?
Ooh, pretty, shiny,
Why is it so fast?
What makes it go?
Never mind, have to
catch it...
up the wall
under the bed
behind the couch
Ha! No fair!
You can't escape
up the curtains
my claws will
see to that...
stupid red light...
I'll get you yet.

Just look what I did
to that toilet roll
who dared challenge
my prowess...
shredded
dissected
its entrails left
in trails
across the floor...
And the newspaper...
oh how it shrieked
as I tore and tussled

and tasted the
black blood ink
of its demise…
One day little light
you too will be mine…

Time to be fussed
stroked and snuggled
my kind and
well-trained human
just loves it
when I jump
onto their lop
or computer
or work papers…
I'm almost sure,
They need a break.
And what better
way to relax
than running fingers
through my fluffy
fur, fabulously fussing
me till I purr
and squiggle my
elastic spine into
the best place,
Go on…
rub my tummy…
I dare you…

Yawn! Oh!
Is it that time?
Already?
I've eaten
and it's been
nearly an hour
since I conquered
the toilet roll,
such a valiant victory.
Must be why
I need a nap
in the last rays
of the sunset.
Wake me,
when it's time
for dinner…

Ink Print

The writer's pen flows freely on the page
leaving marks of truth, image, emotion,
passion and fear, hope, triumph, calm and rage,
all from the artist's mind. Simple notion
formed with simple lines and phrases to fill
a space once blank, devoid of all life, then
with a flurry of motion, then all's still.
Just as night, after the heat of sun, when
exploding again it brings to life
the spirit of all things known to mankind;
sparing express of no joy and no strife…
to tell, to touch, this is the writers' bind;
     their words, their thoughts, shall live forever more,
     ev'ry eye a venue, on e'vry shore.

Tapestry

As the years pass
and the world turns,
we all make mistakes
and we all learn

we each are
single
strands...
amongst a sea
of thread.

Rarely
in our lives
do we really try
to hold on
to what we have,

To fly
As the wind blows...
Change
As the seasons
change,

for change
is what we,
all unknowing...
most dread.

If only we could
Stop

think
amid the worry
and the fuss,
there exists
in this world
7 billion of us.

If we could only
hold on
to one another
we would be twice
as strong as any other.

But we are doomed
forever,
stuck on our own
tiresome tether,
If we remain
single
strands,
one half
without
the other.

In life, we need
only combine,
intertwine,
love
each
other.

Slipping in

So tempting out there, inviting and cool
slowly slipping by, opaque and smooth
a mirror surface, a reflective pool
moving stillness, showing the truth.

A perfect image of all it surrounds,
A sky, stone bridge, dancing leaves
Travel along it, journeys lost and found
losing the edge, to each curve, cleaves.

Like narcissus I yearn to slip in,
like Alice to her wonderland, go far.
Dissolve, and stretch, and grow thin;
lost, reflecting nothing but the stars.

So tempting beyond calling out to me,
Slipping in the river, lost in flow,
No idea where or what I will do or see…
Tempting to be off free, nowhere to go.

Summer Storm

The air is heavy and full of possibility
waiting, tense, anticipating…
I feel it sink into my skin
in the muggy oppressive heat
the feverish thoughts
tied up and snarled together
like tangled rope, strangling me.
That heaviness, inhaled, every breath
makes my chest feel like bursting,
needs to break sometime, doesn't it?

Finally home, momentary shade seems cooler
but shut up windows and doors
mean stale stuffy air until I push the windows
from their panes, out of breath
even if the air outside is hotter.
Clouds are gathering in the dimming light
of the summer sun, trees hold their breath
and I stand still at the open back door
to the night, glass half raised,
waiting, for when it starts to break.

Like the pulse of air, breath, light
Momentarily stops, waits… for… a… beat.
Starting soft, starting slow, like the little
gasp of fear or pain or shock or relief
the first whispers of water kiss the leaves
in my back garden, the calm beginning…
but it won't stay that way, it never does.
Soon the whisper roars and I exhale
in release as I stand in my dry kitchen
staring into the summer storm.

I stare into it a part of and apart from
its energy and drenching influence.
I close my eyes and feel the vibration
of rolling thunder wash through me,
see the flash of lightning despite
eyelids and distance
like the thoughts that race and blow
through my mind, from all corners
the storm rages, turning sighs of relief
from the parched planks into groans
of protest from branches and trunks.

Something resonates in my core, feels the pull
of this chaotic natural burst of water.
Washing the dust and grime
down the cracks that lay beneath
cleansing the surface, sinking in to feed
the thirst of the life left too long
without the clarity of the raging rolling
storm, emptying the pregnant heavy air...
giving birth to something, releasing something,
blanking the slate with air, mind and soul
cleared, for the morning dew.

I'm not to blame!

How could I do *this*?
I'm no carpenter…
No plumber,
No decorator,
No cleaner,
No roofer…
How could I do all that
To keep the house
In order?
That's what the maid
and workmen,
are for,
I'm not responsible.

What am I to do
cold and alone
all day, all night…?
He leaves me untouched
For days…weeks!
I'm only human,
and he was so sweet,
so young,
so handsome,
so attentive…
What am I to do?
If my husband was there
I would never…
It's not my fault!

Everyone else does it,
Calls in sick,
When they're not…
Slips the change
In a pocket,
The economy makes it crazy
Not to take what you can
And my boss is a pig,
Why shouldn't I?
How else can I
Keep up with the neighbours?
It's all so expensive…
Life costs to live,
It's not my fault?

I'm educated, proper
Shouldn't I get more,
Than a bum
Or a foreigner?
I work, pay taxes,
Too much really…
Why shouldn't I
Move to the front
Get tax breaks
Get more benefits
I mean, surely,
I'm worth more
Than the ignorant bum?
Not my responsibility…

Children today…
Ugh…who can control them?
What are their teachers doing?
How can I stop them?
With TV
With movies
With celebrities
With peers
They don't listen!
They're nearly adults
Anyway right?
Society has poisoned
Any chance to reach them
I'm not to blame…

Really???

"Miss! What are we doin' today?"
Doing, it's doing,
You'll find out when we do it...
"Miss! Can you check this please?"
It's one line longer
Than ten minutes ago,
When I checked it
For the fifth time... finish it and I'll check.
"Miss! What do we have to do again?"
I *just* finished telling you...
I love the English language... with all my heart...
Every word... but "MISS!MISS!MISS!"

Miss, thank you for helping me...
Miss, I really love that book,
And I never would have picked it up myself...
Miss, can I help you...
Miss, I never would have passed without you...
Miss, thank you for introducing me to the world of poetry...

OK, maybe, not *so* bad...
Class let's begin...

Motorway Music

Hot and sweating
Beneath the last
Of the summer sun
Looking and lost
For the elusive
Watering hole...pub.

The overpass of M20
Sneaks up so slow
Tired feet crawling
For that blanket
Of shade
On the pavement.

Catch a breath
Catch the shadow
Catch the cool
Surrounding shade
And stop.

Bah-bump bump
Bump bah-bump bump
Tick tick bump
Bah-bump tick
Hisssssss

What is that?
Pause, with the
Water halfway
Raised to drink.

Click, clack
Bah-dum-bump
Tick tick
Hiss bump
Bah-dum-bump

Some workman
Playing the rails?
Some nearby flat
With windows open
In the heat?

Rrrrr, bump, hiss, bump,
Bah-dum-bump,
Bah-dum-bump
Shick shick
Sssszzzzzz
The cars passing
Over my head,
Regulated speed,
Regimental spacing,
Of stabs and seams,
Of tires and transmission.

How have I not
heard it before?
Not noticed the beat?
Not noted the rhythm?
Almost a pulse,
Echoing
In the shade
Underneath.

Commute

The morning is chill; dawn is slow to arrive.
Shades creeping, slow, too slow
for my barely wakeful state.
The fog seems to consume the buildings
Gliding over the river...noiseless
But for the racket
Of the tracks.

There are things, things beside me,
things inside me, my mind,
that I should be taking care of.
Should be... such a vague hovering idea,
Who decided should...?
Whoever it was should shut up,
and pass the coffee, instead of judgment.

In the transition,
Between trains,
Between light and dark,
Between here and there...
A part of me wants to remain.
A part of me always wants to...
Always will do.

On the cusp of things is such a
provocative place,
full of potential energy
potential success
potential failure
potential mystery
potential solutions
potential dreams
potential nightmares
potential anything...

Still...
So still it's like the fog of pre-dawn
Holding its breath.
Then the silence ends,
The train rattles in,
With squeals and squeaks
Shrieks and shuffles...sssssssss.....
As it stops.

On to the next transition.

Moments of Transition

There is a time between times when
holding your breath feels right, before
a change in the air, mind, light…then
exhale to the moment soak in more.
Waiting for rain the air is dense, full.
A metallic tang you can feel, taste
building, pressing a tactile pull
like a diver in vast empty space.
The cusp of day, beginnings and ends,
anticipation or regret hang there
in transition as time wends
its immutable way to flare
in the guttering candle of a star
or the sleepy sigh of another
stretched out with the speed of tar
in the sliding tear that just covers
the tipping point of our days…
transitions never helping or hinting
At the multitude of ways
The never quite here seems to be glinting.

Winter Dawn

A muffled silence greets the first grey beams
Where floating flakes of frozen lacework fall
Softly, silently, and a whisper seems
As loud and lairy as a legion call.
Still blinking with sleep, slipping from the warm
Into the crisp air at the cusp of day,
With thoughts thickened trying to take some form,
Gazing on frozen beauty, nought to say
But breathe in the metallic taste of air,
Soaking in the sound of no sound at all,
Waiting and wishing the world was as clear,
As this winter's dawn, and this first snow fall.
      This peace of this perfect moment, shine alone,
      When I hold the memory I'm back home.

Incense and Time

The heavy weight of the door gives me pause,
As if I need to brace thoughts, or shoulder...
Coloured light that greets me shows me the cause,
Looking I suddenly feel much older.
Solid beams weighed close, centuries of time,
Solid walls hold fast years of solid faith,
I feel belonging in a place not mine,
Anticipation of grace, fear the wait.
Saturating the air, spiced scent breeds calm,
Warmth of close candles folds the skin in peace,
Quiet prayers, thoughts of hope act as a balm,
This place of incense and time without cease.
        Back out in the sun, seeming a new sight
        I step lighter with soul made fresh and light.

Thank You For Remembering

I know you know me far, far too well…
My heart, my mind, the feelings I never, ever, tell.
You know the little things I can't let anyone know,
The ground hidden places, where my dreams grow.
You remember my hopes, and what touches me deep,
When you look in my eyes, no secret can I keep.
I can only say, thank you for remembering
The simple things, your own pure rendering.
I'm speechless in surprise, it's always there,
No matter what you, my friend, somehow, always care.

I know you're here, no matter what to comfort me,
Because you've been there many times before.
If all who know you, could see what I see,
I know, unanimous, they would be sure.

You carry happiness, every time you laugh,
You close the notebook, shut away pain that's past.
Every gesture you make, seeks to make me smile,
A true friend strong enough to go the full mile.
You read the whole story, joy and sorrows.
I hope you're part of me now and all my tomorrows.
Thank you for remembering, knowing me better than I.
I'll never be able, no matter how hard I try,
To tell you, in days and nights, through and through
I never would have made it without friends like you.

Ready... Just

I'm ready for things
to be just a little
easier...
not easy...
just...
easier.

I'm ready for nights
to be a little less
dark...
not bright...
just...
lighter.

I'm ready for days
to be just a little
calmer
not boring...
just...
calmer.

I'm ready for people
to be just a little
kinder...
not pushovers...
just...
kinder.

I'm ready for love
to be just a little
closer...
not invasive...
just...
closer.

I'm ready for fear
to be a little less
crippling...
not oblivious
just...
manageable.

I'm ready for time
to move just a little
slower...
not tedious
just...
slower.

I'm ready for confidence
to be just a little
stronger...
not arrogant
just...
stronger.

I'm ready for choices
to be a little
clearer...
not predestined
just...
clearer.

I'm ready for consequences
to be a little less
irrevocable
not forgotten
just easier
to remedy.

4-° 12' 2-" N 7-° 4' 2-" W

Solid, old...for my country anyway...
Even lines of cladding, like ribs or a xylophone,
Green rough tiles, pebbly under my feet
When I clean the gutters of autumn leaves.

Three floors packed to the rafters
With memories and moments
With dishes and do's and don'ts
With wishes and will's and won'ts.

A picket fence...(no really... a picket fence)
Surrounding the dog's yard.
Sadly without the dog for many years.

100 year old barn topped up with treasures
Every time my dad gave in to going to an auction.
Summer weekends
Trying to sell on
Auction treasures
with 'garage' sales
and lemonade stands.

Three cars on the drive, one under a sheet...
Gardens and trees, as old as the house... older
Pushing at the picket fence.

In the backyard the haven of my youth,
The true draw to parties...the swimming pool.
Cannon balls and dunking extraordinaire;
Sun bathing on concrete and floating chairs.

Up the back steps,
(the front is for strangers and guests)
The door is almost never locked...
Screen door creaks just so,
The inner door, squeeze, lift and
bump once or twice
with the hip, it sticks.

The 45s juke box on the inside back porch
Many, many music video worthy
performances
Dancing and singing at the top
Of our unashamed ten year old voices.
Not understanding lyrics,
But loving the tunes anyway.

Onward
Inside a second, creakier door,
The family room, only a decade older
than I am.
Lazy Saturdays, afternoon cartoons...
Early sneak peaks of Christmas morning...
A couch for sinking into,
For old movies with mom,
Slumber parties with the girls,
Or a first, shy kiss...
Parents just through the ceiling.

Next the kitchen, centre of the house...
Literally,
Figuratively,
Actually.

Baking a multitude of cookies,
Every Christmas.
Dozens of turkeys
For Thanksgivings
Of varying sizes,
Depending on guests…
Blood related…
Or otherwise.

I remember the old cracked box
Containing the yellowed and stained
Family recipes… filed incomprehensibly.
Brought out at need,
Along with inherited recipe books
Stacked and squished, above the sink,
Next to battered measuring cups
That no one makes anymore.

I got the 'yucky' jobs, mixing eggs
Into dough, with bare hands.
Helping sprinkle coloured sugar
Onto butter cookies,
That didn't have many ingredients,
Besides butter.
Helping and learning,
Loving and growing.
A well-oiled sous chef to my mother,
Before I knew what such a thing was.

Carrying platter after plate,
to the dining room.

Like going back in time,
oldest part of the house.
Punched tin chandelier, candles aglow,
Above an oak table that always seemed,
Somehow,
To be big enough
for whomever joined us.

Pewter plates, depression-ware glasses
(from grandmother)
A place for everything,
Just,
In a room that always felt warm,
And full,
But never,
Too small.

The front room,
My favourite place.
Grandfather's player piano,
Shelf after shelf of player piano scrolls…
Songs I never knew, played
As if by ghosts,
(Friendly ones)
As my ten year old feet
Pumped the pedals,
When tired of practicing
My scales.

Walls so covered in family photos
Of previous generations,
And our own,

Till almost no wall
Can be seen
For the faces.
Shelves of photo albums
(for the run over)
Of baby pictures,
Passed away pets,
Glorious
Happy
Childhoods.
Footprints and hair clippings
For each child.
Was my hair ever that colour?

Like a sanctuary,
My sanctuary,
With antique books,
A soft radio,
A colonial woodstove,
Dim, unobtrusive light
to read by.
The modern world
And its modern demands,
Slips away, and I am left,
Wrapped in family,
In blankets,
With hot chocolate,
and peace of soul.

Up the stairs, with its bannister
coming away from the wall,
but never detached.

The wobble of loose screws
Somehow comforting,
Rather than concerning.

My bedroom to the left,
Another to the right,
Once brother's.
A lofted bed
Man cave under it;
Comics and bookshelves
From which I 'borrowed'
And read tales
Till they literally
Fell apart to be
Taped up, to read again.

A forbidden zone,
Except when they needed
To sneak 'Santa's' presents
Out of the attic
Above my own.
That night I was 'allowed',
In a conspiracy of magic,
To believe a little longer...
Part of me always will.

Eventually sister's,
Plush, pink pastel.
Disney and dancing
To pop music,
Till I wanted
To bury my head

In pillows, escape
One more round,
Of 'I'm a Barbie Girl'.
Rooms on rotation as growing
Set our paths from home.

My room, changed and yet not,
Whenever I go home.
Lovingly made shelves,
overflowing with antique toys,
keepsakes and collectables,
line the circumference
of my ceiling.
A rope bed, uncomfortable,
Creaky, centuries out of fashion.
I would cry if they replaced it.
Hand stencilled tulips,
By my mother's hand,
on wooden floor boards
and walls, matching mauve
doors and trim.
Never liked pink…but could never
Give that up.

Treasures, gathered and kept.
Toys and trends,
teddy bears, tickets,
pogs, pond stones,
necklaces and knick-knacks…
till every corner
is crowded with clutter,
and each piece

a memory,
revisited at view
or when cleaning…
newly discovered
at every dusting,
as if lived that moment.

Somehow, we never fought
Over the bathroom,
With its clawfoot tub,
And with tricky electrics…
For the hair dryer,
that would blow the fuse,
if too many lights,
or TVs,
Were on at the same time.
Howling from every corner
At who was responsible…

The hallway had its charms,
The sewing machine,
Antique
No fancy patterns
Or multiple
Settings
Yet still…
Off of it came
Halloween costumes
Out of a little girl's
Fairytale dreams.
A jar of buttons,

Saved by grandmother,
Because in the depression,
With six girls,
You threw away nothing.
Creaking floorboards,
And dim lights,
Of proud
Parent displayed
Childrens' drawings
And gifts of poems.
Too much like hallmark cards
Before I wrote my own.

The 'nursery',
or computer room,
Or guest room,
Depending on the rota
Of growing up,
Grandmother's bed,
From those last years,
Still makes me smile,
Feel like she's there.

My parents' room,
Safe place,
Where I can
Lay on dad's shoulder
Or play with mom's hair,
Till sleep keeps me safe
From monsters,
And the dark.

From thunder,
From loneliness.
Sleeping on the floor,
When the dark,
Got too dark,
Till the nightlight,
was more than enough,
and reading
just one more page,
became more enticing.

It wasn't just the dark...
There were the scary parts,
The basement...
Where I ran in...
And out... only as absolutely
Necessary.
The attic... that was haunted,
No matter what
My mother tried to tell me.
Especially at night,
Especially by the door,
That opens
Into my room
When I'm not
Looking,
I'm sure...

The attic
Tamed by mom
With a playroom

Where I joined in the conspiracy,
Much later,
Wrapping 'Santa's' presents
Once it was my turn,
To keep my sister's faith,
A little longer.

But between the scary parts,
A fortress of love,
Like life,
Stumbling in innocence
And ignorance,
With only home
As a touch stone.

Summers peeling corn,
On the back steps.
Dog going crazy,
In the yard,
Scaring rabbits
And town kids…
More terrier
Than terrifying
Not that she knew.
Memorial day parades,
First watching in childhood,
Not understood
then performed.
Before or after
My birthdays
Topped

With mom's strawberry shortcake,
As only she can make it.
With barbeques by the pool,
Running through sprinklers
And backyards
Playing tag,
And manhunt,
Until it's too dark
Or the voices
Call us home
For dinner.

Autumns decorating the 'graveyard'
Spreading spiderwebs,
Lighting candles,
Sneaking sweets.
Spilling secrets, so the 'witch'
Could tell, my friend's fortunes
With mysterious accuracy.
How they never
Caught on,
I'll never know.
Or maybe they did,
But pretended…
The magic of
The witching hour.
Crunching leaves of every colour,
Piled high and that smell…
Nothing like that smell…
Not good, not bad,
Fresh and natural.

Shifting sounds
Cicadas in the wind,
Having left their alien shells
Hanging, lifelike, from the bark.
New school year,
new challenges
with the energy growing,
as the light dims.

Winters by the fire places,
Smelling wood smoke,
Knowing warmth, watching snow,
Hibernating.
Sledging down
The small hill,
Down the road.
Drying mittens
And socks
And numb fingers
on the grate of the fireplace.
Crackling and ash,
Glow and embers,
Like magic, like tongues
Licking my clothes,
In the same way
It licks the wood
in the grate.
The smell of baking,
And cooking,
Filling the house,
For what seems like

A month.
Between Thanksgiving
And Christmas…
Between friends and family
The warmth of company
Chasing out the cold
Of the outside,
Hot chocolate,
Jell-O in antique glasses
And mulled wine.
Board games that end
In peals of laughter,
No matter who wins,
If anyone is even
Keeping score.

Springs of hidden Easter eggs
Dyed the day before,
Crayola crayons
Making faces and animals,
Patterns, in boiling water
And vinegar…
The distinctive smell
Forever associated
With the kitchen
And spring,
Even now…
Decades and miles away.
Eating baskets of sweets,
Trading for our favourites.
Sugar highs for days.

Floor boards
To ceiling beams,
Broken bricks
In kitchen
Or walkway,
To ancient sash windows,
Iron radiators
That click
And creak
To keep warm.
Modern conveniences
Buried under
Mountains of antiques,
Ages of family
Collected,
Surrounding,
In my home...

A harbour from heartbreak,
A classroom of wisdom,
A place of belonging,
A dream and a bastion
For all we could become,
And all we must remember to be,
Set the compass,
Set the course,
Let me never forget.

The coordinates of home.

Acknowledgments

I want to thank my friends and family who have walked beside me and made this book possible. To Janet and Louis Pacchioli, my parents, you were my first and best teachers for all the things school couldn't teach. I also want to thank *all* my teachers, past and present, who taught me to love the written word and that my voice had value. In particular Mr Abel, who I still don't feel right calling by his first name... you are the English teacher I strive to be...and yes you can deduct two points for that, they're worth it.

I would like to thank the team at Conscious Dreams Publishing; Nadia Vitushynska, my typesetter and Daniella Blechner, my editor and Book Journey Mentor for helping something I've dreamed of for so long to become more than a dream. Thank you to my friend and colleague, Julie Smith, for introducing me to them.

About the Author

 Raised in the US but living in the UK for nearly half her life, Leah has a complex perspective on the world around her. Identifying as a teacher, a writer and academic Leah has been writing poetry and fiction for more than 20 years, hoping to pin her emotions and experiences to the page and share them with others.

Teaching for nine years has taught her that people all feel alone and isolated at some point, even in a crowd... so Leah attempts to reach out with her poems to let others know they are not alone.

Leah holds degrees in English, Comparative Literature and International Studies from Pennsylvania State University in the United States as well as a Minor in German Language and Literature. At Canterbury Christ Church University Leah trained for a PGCE in teaching secondary English, Media Studies and Drama.

Most days are spent sharing her passion for the written word with young people, trying to comprehend British slang and making sure her coffee cup is never empty for the health and safety of others. She resides in Wimbledon, always looking for inspiration.

Conscious Dreams
P U B L I S H I N G

Be the author of your own destiny

Find out about our authors, events, services
and how you too can get your book journey started.

Conscious Dreams Publishing

@DreamsConscious

@consciousdreamspublishing

Daniella Blechner

www.consciousdreamspublishing.com

info@consciousdreamspublishing.com

Let's connect